Sara Swan Miller

Owls

The Silent Hunters

Franklin Watts - A Division of Grolier Publishing
New York • London • Hong Kong • Sydney • Danbury, Connecticut

For Marty
Who cooks for YOU? Who cooks for YOU-all?

Photographs ©: Animals Animals: 43 (Bill Beatty), 13 (Ken Cole), 15 (Breck P. Kent), 17 (Zig Leszczynski); BBC Natural History Unit: 25 (Niall Benvie), 5 bottom right (Kevin J. Keatley), 5 bottom left (Mary Ann McDonald), 7 (Dietmar Nill), 5 top left (Tom Vezo); Kevin Schafer: 21; Photo Researchers: 5 top right (E. R. Degginger), 27 (Fletcher & Baylis), 31 (David Hosking), 41 (Jeff Lepore), 29 (Anthony Mercieca), 35 (A. H. Rider), 23 (Len Rue Jr.); Tony Stone Images: 42 (Daniel J. Cox), 37 (Manfred Danneger), cover (Tim Davis), 33 (David E. Myers), 1 (Art Wolfe); Visuals Unlimited: 39 (Stephen J. Lang), 19 (Gary Meszaros), 6 (Rob Simpson).

Illustrations by Jose Gonzales and Steve Savage

The photo on the cover shows a great horned owl. The photo on the title page shows a group of screech owlets.

Visit Franklin Watts on the Internet at:
http://publishing.grolier.com

Library of Congress Cataloging-in-Publication Data

Miller, Sara Swan.
Owls, the silent hunters / Sara Swan Miller.
      p. cm. — (Animals in order)
   Includes bibliographical references and index.
   Summary: Describes the general physical characteristics and behavior of owls and takes an in-depth look at fourteen different species.
      ISBN 0-531-11595-X (lib. bdg.)   0-531-16496-9 (pbk.)
   Owls—juvenile literature. [1. Owls.] I. Title. II. Series.
QL696.S8 M57   2000
598.9'7 21—dc21   99-042008

© 2000 Franklin Watts, a division of Grolier Publishing
All rights reserved. Published simultaneously in Canada.
Printed in the United States of America.
1 2 3 4 5 6 7 8 9 10 R 09 08 07 06 05 04 03 02 01 00

Contents

Is That an Owl?

Owls are birds of mystery. These silent hunters lead secret lives. They usually hide during the day and come out at dawn and dusk. You may have never seen an owl in the wild. Their feathers help them blend in with their surroundings. During the day, they sit silent and still on their *roosts*, so they are hard to spot. At night, they fly so quietly that not even a sharp-eared mouse can hear them. Only an owl's mysterious cries let you know when one is nearby.

If you ever see an owl, you'll recognize it right away. It sits upright on its perch, looking almost as if it has no head. It turns its flat face around and looks in every direction with its big, round eyes.

Owls have other things in common too. Look at the pictures of owls on the next page. How are owls different from other birds?

Great horned owl

Eastern screech owl

Snowy owl

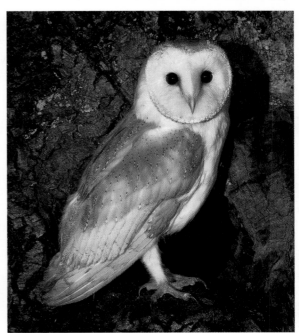

Barn owl

Traits of Owls

An owl's eyes are on the front of its head.

Most owls hunt in the dim light of dusk and dawn. They are well suited to the life they lead. In the evening, they can see 10 to 100 times better than humans can. They also see perfectly well in the daylight. The eyes of most birds are on the sides of their head, but an owl's eyes are in front. They can use both eyes together to track their *prey*. Forward-facing eyes also give owls good *depth perception*.

An owl's eyes are fixed—they can't move in their sockets. To watch a moving object, an owl must turn its entire head. The bones in an owl's neck make it possible for the bird to rotate its head almost all the way around.

An owl has huge ears inside its large, wide head. Most owls have one ear set higher than the other, so they can locate the exact spot where their prey is hiding. Their flat disk-shaped face can "catch" sounds and reflect them to their ears.

Owls fly so silently that the animals they hunt almost never hear them coming. An owl's feathers are covered with soft furry down that muffles any sound. The feathers along the front edge of an owl's wings look as though they have been thinned out with scissors. Because the wings have no hard edges, they do not make the whooshing sound that you hear when other birds fly. Many owls also have feathers on their legs, which make them even quieter in flight.

An owl grabs prey with its big, strong *talons*. If the animal is small enough, the owl gulps it down whole. If the animal is large, the owl uses its sharp, hooked beak to tear the prey into pieces.

This owl is about to catch a mouse.

The Order of Living Things

A tiger has more in common with a house cat than with a daisy. A true bug is more like a butterfly than a jellyfish. Scientists arrange living things into groups based on how they look and how they act. A tiger and a house cat belong to the same group, but a daisy belongs to a different group.

Sponges Cnidarians Flatworms Roundworms Arthropods Annelids Mollusks Echinoderms

Animals

Plants Fungi

Monerans Protists

All living things can be placed in one of five groups called *kingdoms*: the plant kingdom, the animal kingdom, the fungus kingdom, the moneran kingdom, or the protist kingdom. You can probably name many of the creatures in the plant and animal kingdoms. The fungus kingdom includes mushrooms, yeasts, and molds. The moneran and protist kingdoms contain thousands of living things that are too small to see without a microscope.

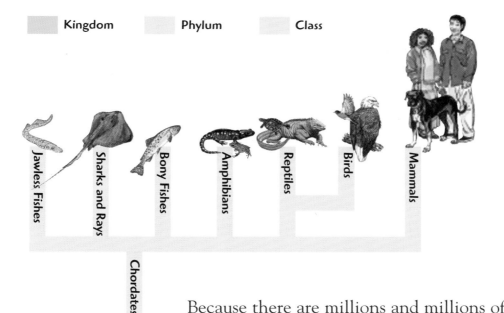

Kingdom   Phylum   Class

Jawless Fishes

Sharks and Rays

Bony Fishes

Amphibians

Reptiles

Birds

Mammals

Chordates

Because there are millions and millions of living things on Earth, some of the members of one kingdom may not seem all that similar. The animal kingdom includes creatures as different as tarantulas and trout, jellyfish and jaguars, salamanders and sparrows, elephants and earthworms.

To show that an elephant is more like a jaguar than an earthworm, scientists further separate the creatures in each kingdom into more specific groups. The animal kingdom can be divided into nine *phyla*. Humans belong to the chordate phylum. Almost all chordates have a backbone.

Each phylum can be subdivided into many *classes*. Humans, mice, and elephants all belong to the mammal class. Each class can be further divided into *orders*; orders into *families*, families into *genera*, and genera into *species*. All the members of a species are very similar.

How Owls Fit In

You can probably guess that owls belong to the animal kingdom. They have much more in common with spiders and snakes than with maple trees and morning glories.

Owls belong in the chordate phylum. Almost all chordates have a backbone and a skeleton. Can you think of other chordates? Examples include elephants, mice, snakes, frogs, fish, and whales.

All birds belong to the same class. There are about thirty different orders of birds. Owls make up one of these orders.

Owls are divided into a number of different families and genera. These groups can be broken down into about 170 species. Some owls are thought of as pests because they occasionally kill chickens or other farm animals, but those same species eat great numbers of insects, mice, and rats.

Owls live in all parts of the world so, no matter where you live, there are probably owls close by. In this book, you will learn more about fourteen species of owls.

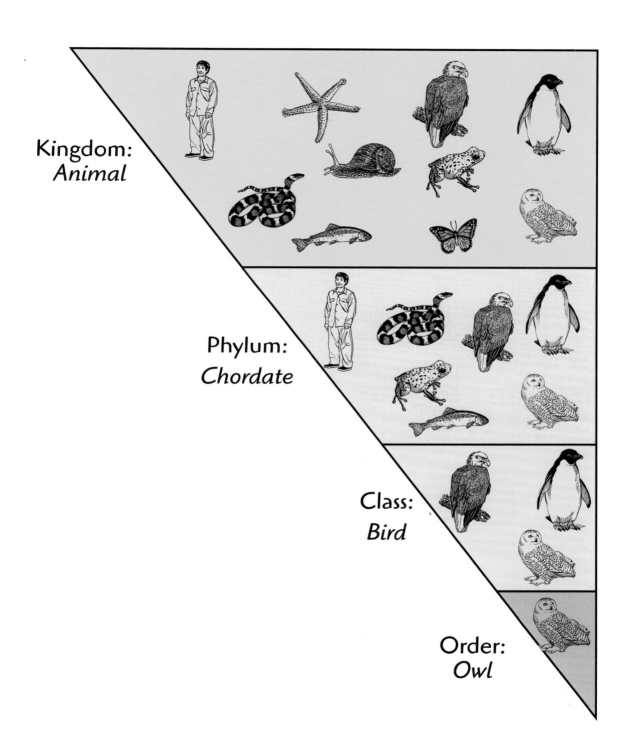

Kingdom: *Animal*

Phylum: *Chordate*

Class: *Bird*

Order: *Owl*

Eagle Owls

FAMILY: Strigidae
COMMON EXAMPLE: Great horned owl
GENUS AND SPECIES: *Bubo virginianus*
SIZE: 18 to 25 inches (46 to 63.5 cm)

As dusk falls, a great horned owl sits perched on a branch that overlooks a darkening meadow. The owl turns its head around, back and forth. It is looking and listening for signs of prey. Is that a mouse sneaking through the grass?

The owl bobs its head up and down and slides it from side to side. This helps the giant bird pinpoint the mouse's exact location. The owl drops from its perch, swoops low, and grabs the mouse with its talons, killing it instantly. In one gulp, the mouse is gone.

The owl returns to its perch and lets out a loud cry. On a still night, the great horned owl's hoot can be heard for several miles. It can also mee-oo-ow like a cat and bark like a dog. The great horned owl can even throw its voice, so the sound seems to come from a different place.

The great horned owl gets its name from the large tufts of feathers on top of its head. Some people think these tufts look like horns.

Great horned owls are found all over North and South America. In many places, they're the kind of owl you are most likely to see. What is the secret of their success? They're great hunters, and they eat many different kinds of animals. They feed on mice, rats, rabbits,

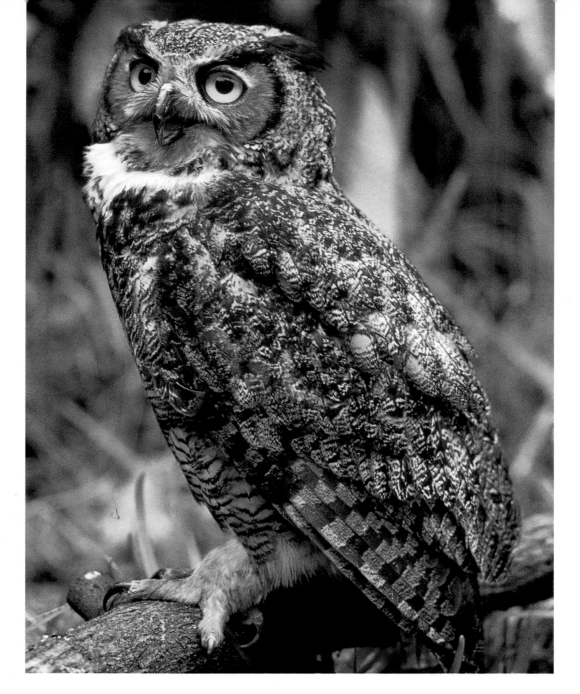

ground squirrels, and opossums. They also eat other birds, including ducks and geese. They'll even eat skunks. A skunk's smelly defense doesn't seem to help when a great horned owl wants a meal.

Wood Owls

FAMILY: Strigidae
COMMON EXAMPLE: Barred owl
GENUS AND SPECIES: *Strix varia*
SIZE: 16 to 25 inches (41 to 63.5 cm)

A barred owl perches quietly on a tree branch in the deep woods. As it waits for nightfall, the owl sits close to the trunk. The bird's brownish-gray feathers help it blend in with the tree. If you walked under the tree, you probably wouldn't even notice the owl.

Suddenly, a flock of crows discovers the *predator*. They fly at and around the owl, cawing loudly and making a terrible racket. The owl is alarmed and confused. It stretches up tall, so its body looks like an upright branch. The crows aren't fooled, though. They keep cawing and attacking. Finally, the owl has had enough and flies away.

Crows seem to know that owls mean danger. Whenever they come across one, they *mob* it loudly. If you hear crows making a racket out in the woods, go take a look. You may find an owl at the center of the upset. Jays and chickadees may also mob a roosting owl during the day, scolding loudly to drive it away.

Listen for barred owls calling in the woods, especially on late-winter evenings. It sounds as though they're saying, "Who cooks for YOU? Who cooks for YOU-all?"

Screech Owls

FAMILY: Strigidae
COMMON EXAMPLE: Eastern screech owl
GENUS AND SPECIES: *Otus asio*
SIZE: 8 to10 inches (20 to 25 cm)

In early spring, a male screech owl finds an old woodpecker hole. It will make a perfect nest site. He leaves mice and other tasty food inside to attract a mate.

When a female discovers the nest hole, the male begins to *court* her. He lets out a high, eerie call, bows, and spreads his wings. Soon the two owls are sitting side by side and *preening* each other's head feathers.

After the female lays her eggs, she sits on them until the chicks hatch a month later. All this time, the male keeps her supplied with food. When the chicks hatch, they have no feathers. The female continues to sit on the nest to keep the hatchlings warm. The male brings his family food. The female tears the prey into small bits for the very young birds.

When the owlets finally leave the nest, they still can't fly. They use their bills, talons, and wings to climb about in their tree. The protective parents watch the young owls closely. If an enemy gets to too close, the female may swoop down at it.

Little Owls

FAMILY: Strigidae
COMMON EXAMPLE: Burrowing owl
GENUS AND SPECIES: *Speotyto cunicularia*
SIZE: 8 1/2 to 11 inches (21.5 to 28 cm)

Most burrowing owls don't dig their own burrows. They just move into a burrow that has been dug by a prairie dog, a ground squirrel, or another animal. These owls don't build a nest inside, but sometimes they line the burrow with cow manure. They like the softness and don't seem to mind the smell.

The burrowing owl's habit of taking over other animals' burrows led to a problem in Florida not long ago. People who were planning to build a new sports stadium dug a number of holes in the ground to test the *soil* for pollution. Guess who moved in? Since Florida law protects burrowing owls, building the stadium had to wait until the owls had raised their young and left the area.

Like many kinds of owls, burrowing owls hunt mostly in the evening and at night. In the spring, when a male is feeding his mate and chicks, he also hunts during the day. Burrowing owls have many different hunting methods. They may snap up flying insects in the air, run along the ground to catch mice and other small mammals, or perch on a tree and swoop down on their prey. Sometimes they even hover over the fields searching for lizards and snakes.

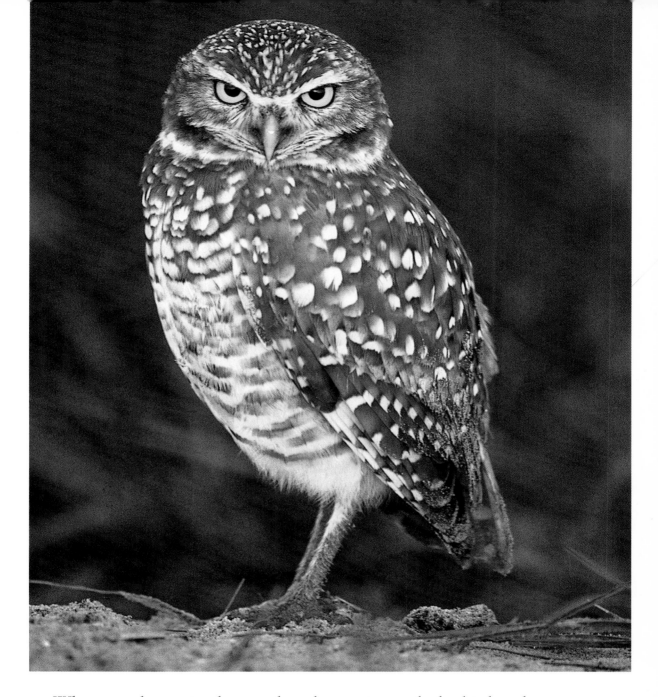

When another animal passes by a burrowing owl, the bird nods as if it were saying "hello." That's why cowboys used to call these little owls "howdy" birds.

Spectacled Owls

FAMILY: Strigidae
COMMON EXAMPLE: Spectacled owl
GENUS AND SPECIES: *Pulsatrix perspicillata*
SIZE: 18 inches (46 cm)

Can you guess how a spectacled owl got its name? The white markings around its eyes make this bird look as though it's wearing glasses. A young spectacled owl looks very different from its parents. It has white feathers on its body and a dark face mask. People often call the owlets "white owls," thinking they're a different species. Almost 5 years pass before the owlets look like their parents.

Spectacled owls live mostly in dense, tropical rain forests. They hunt at night and hide during the day, so they're hard to spot. The only way you might know they're around is by their strange call. The female has a hawk-like scream that some people say sounds like a steam whistle. Both males and females make a series of tapping "pops" that sound a lot like a woodpecker at work on a tree. In Brazil, spectacled owls are known as "knocking owls."

Like many other owls, spectacled owls nest in tree holes. But they usually don't build a nest inside. If another bird has made a nest, they'll use it. Otherwise, the female just lays her eggs on the bare floor of the hole or in sawdust that has piled up.

Spectacled owls lay only two eggs, but those owlets keep their parents busy. The adults start bringing small mammals, insects, and

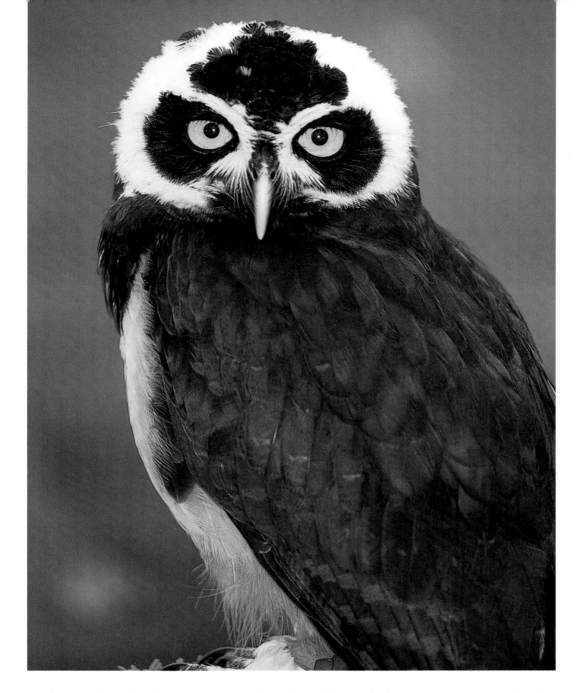

crabs to the chicks as soon as they hatch, and they continue to feed the owlets for a long time. Even though young owls leave the nest soon after they hatch, they can't fly until they're about 1 year old.

Eagle Owls

FAMILY: *Strigidae*
COMMON NAME: Eurasian eagle owl
GENUS AND SPECIES: *Bubo bubo*
SIZE: 26 to 28 inches (66 to 71 cm)

"Hoo, hoo." A male eagle owl is telling other owls, "Go away! This is my *territory*." He doesn't want to share the prey in his territory.

Even though it's very early in the spring, the eagle owl is ready to start a family. He and his mate have found an old eagle's nest. While the male is busy scaring away strangers, the female is busy laying eggs. She sits on the eggs for more than a month. All that time, the male brings her food. When the chicks hatch, he brings mice, birds, and other prey to his family.

After 5 weeks, the owlets are ready to leave the nest. The parents' work isn't done, though. Several months will pass before the young can fly well enough to hunt for their own food. They need a lot of practice before they become expert hunters. Because young eagle owls hatch in early spring, they have the whole summer to learn how to hunt.

Eurasian eagle owls are the biggest owls in the world, with a wingspan of 5 feet (1.5 m). They have giant, powerful talons and a heavy, eaglelike bill. Although they usually eat *rodents* and birds, they also hunt larger animals, including foxes and porcupines. They can even attack a small deer four times their weight!

22

Wood Owls

FAMILY: Strigidae
COMMON EXAMPLE: Tawny owl
GENUS AND SPECIES: *Strix aluco*
SIZE: 15 inches (38 cm)

Tawny owls are often heard, but rarely seen. They hunt in the deep dark of night, swooping silently over the fields. During the day, they hide in tree holes or perch on a branch close to the trunk of a tree. Their feathers are just the right colors to blend with their surroundings. At night, you can hear female tawny owls calling "to-whit" and the males answering "to-whoo."

You might also hear the owlets begging for food with their hissing "shee-ep, shee-ep." Their parents usually feed them rodents, but sometimes they hunt hedgehogs, frogs, or worms. At dawn or dusk, they may catch other birds. Their short, curved claws are good for snatching birds in midair.

In some places, tawny owls share their territory with Ural owls and the great grey owls. How do they manage to get along? Most of the time, different species hunt at different times. Great grey owls often hunt during the day, while the Ural owls prefer dusk, and tawny owls hunt only at night.

Tawny owls and Ural owls do compete for nesting sites, though. They both like nesting in tree holes. Sometimes Ural owls solve this problem very simply—they just eat the smaller tawny owls.

Fish Owls

FAMILY: Strigidae
COMMON EXAMPLE: Buffy fish owl
GENUS AND SPECIES: *Ketupa ketupu*
SIZE: 16 1/2 inches (42 cm)

As dusk falls in a Malaysian rain forest, a buffy fish owl flies out of the dense woods where it has been hiding all day. The owl settles on a stump that leans over a river, peers into the water, and watches for fish.

Suddenly, the bird spots a fish. It is just below the surface of the water. The owl swoops down, snatches the fish in its talons, and carries the struggling prey back to its roost. The fish becomes a one-gulp meal.

Buffy fish owls are well suited to a fish-eating life. Their legs are featherless, and they have sharp, spiky scales on the undersides of their feet. Their talons are long and curved with sharp, cutting edges. Those feet let buffy fish owls hold onto a slippery fish no matter how hard it wriggles.

Unlike other owls, buffy fish owls don't fly silently. That doesn't matter, though. Fish can't hear them, even if they are very noisy. Buffy fish owls are different from most other owls in another way too. They don't have a disk-shaped face to help them hear. These birds don't use their ears to find fish. They rely entirely on their keen eyes.

Sometimes fish owls wade in shallow water. Usually, they're just bathing, but if they come upon a crayfish or a crab, they'll snatch it right up. Any creature it finds in the water makes a tasty meal for a fish owl.

Scops Owls

FAMILY: Strigidae
COMMON EXAMPLE: White-faced scops owl
GENUS AND SPECIES: *Otus leucotis*
SIZE: 11 inches (28 cm)

White-faced scops owls live in the grasslands and thorn scrubs of Africa. Their most notable features are their long "ear tufts." Actually, these aren't ears at all. They're just big tufts of feathers. They help the owl blend in with its surroundings.

It's hard to sneak up on one of these owls. It will hear you and see you long before you spot it. When a white-faced scops owl feels threatened, it freezes instantly in an upright position. With its feathers sleeked down and its ear tufts sticking up, it looks more like a broken branch than an owl. If you do get close to a white-faced scops owl, it may fly away, or it may open its orange eyes wide and snap its bill at you.

Most of the time, these small owls hunt at night. They eat insects, small rodents, and young birds. Other birds seem to know that white-faced scops owls are a threat. If ravens or starlings come across a roosting owl, they mob it—shrieking and flying at it—until it flies off and leaves their chicks in peace.

Southern Hawk Owls

FAMILY: Strigidae
COMMON EXAMPLE: Boobook
GENUS AND SPECIES: *Ninox novaeseelandiae*
SIZE: 10 1/2 to 14 inches (27 to 35.5 cm)

If you ever hear a boobook, you'll know how it got its name. Its most common call is "Boobook! Boobook!" This owl is more often heard than it is seen. People who live in Australia often hear males in the woods at night, warning away intruders.

Boobooks have other calls too. Sometimes males and females get into what sounds like a conversation, chattering in low tones back and forth. At other times they sound like stray cats howling as they prowl in the darkness.

Boobooks don't have disk-shaped faces, so they don't hear as well as other owls. Boobooks are also different from other owls in another way. They don't have one ear set higher than the other. As a result, they have trouble pinpointing the exact location of scurrying prey.

Even though boobooks don't hear as well as some owls, they still hunt at night. They rely on their excellent eyesight to spot prey. Imagine flying over an area the size of a football field on a dark night and trying to spot a mouse. Do you think you'd be able to do it? Probably not, but a boobook could.

Snowy Owls

FAMILY: Strigidae
COMMON NAME: Snowy owl
GENUS AND SPECIES: *Nyctea scandiaca*
SIZE: 20 to 27 inches (51 to 68.5 cm)

You can guess where snowy owls live by looking at their feathers. They live far north on the Arctic *tundra*, where their white bodies blend in with the snowy landscape. Their thick feathers, which grow all the way down to their toes, keep them warm in the coldest weather.

In the far north, the summer nights are very short. That's why snowy owls do most of their hunting during the day. They perch in trees and swoop down on lemmings and other rodents. In the winter, they move a little farther south and hunt rabbits, ground squirrels, and even birds as large as geese.

In early spring, a male starts defending his territory with deep booming hoots. When a female appears, he flies in with long, slow wing beats and drops a lemming at her feet. He lands on the ground next to her, leans forward, and raises his wings. You might imagine that he's saying "Here's a nice lemming for you."

The female chooses a snow-free spot with a good view of the area and scrapes out a shallow nest for her eggs. While she sits on the nest to keep the eggs warm, the male brings her food. After about a month, the chicks hatch. Even after the young owls leave the nest,

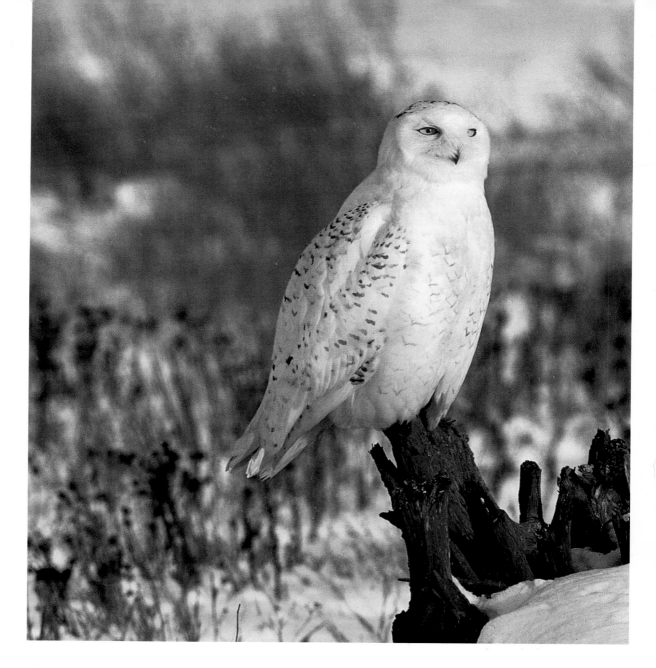

their parents still feed them. After about 10 weeks, the owlets begin to fly and hunt on their own.

In years when lemmings are scarce, snowy owls don't have any young. Maybe that's one reason people think of owls as wise.

Forest Owls

FAMILY: Strigidae
COMMON NAME: Boreal owl
GENUS AND SPECIES: *Aegolius funereus*
SIZE: 10 inches (25 cm)

It is a cold winter night in a dense northern forest. More than 24 inches (61 cm) of snow cover the ground. A boreal owl sits on a branch, looking and listening for the slightest sign of prey. Suddenly, the owl hears a tiny sound. The bird sticks out its neck and turns its disk-shaped face toward the noise.

The owl leaps from its perch and swoops toward the sound. Chest first, the owl flops on the snow, wings and tail spread. It heaves its body up and down, and then sits up with a vole in its talons. The bird stuffs the prey in its beak and swallows it in two gulps. Imagine being able to hear a tiny vole that's buried under so much snow!

In the spring, you can hear a male boreal owl defending his territory. He calls out with a quick, constant "coo-coo-coo-coo-coo-coo." The male flies from tree hole to tree hole, singing away and showing his mate good nest sites. Finally, she chooses one and lays her eggs.

Four weeks later, the first chicks begin to hatch. By the time the last owlets come out of their eggs, the first ones are already getting big. Sometimes there isn't enough food to go around. Then the youngest owlets die, leaving the older ones to share whatever food their parents can find.

Barn and Grass Owls

FAMILY: Tytonidae
COMMON EXAMPLE: Barn owl
GENUS AND SPECIES: *Tyto alba*
SIZE: 12 1/2 to 16 inches (32 to 41 cm)

A barn owl has a white, heart-shaped face. Because this owl has pale coloring and sometimes nests in church steeples, some people call it the ghost owl or the church owl. During the day, you might come across one of these owls roosting in a barn or in a tree. It will probably hear you coming before you see it, though, and fly away on soundless wings.

A barn owl hunts at night, swooping low over open fields. Its hearing is so good that its ears can detect the sound of a mouse pattering through the grass. The moment it locates prey, the barn owl drops down suddenly and lets out a strange, raspy shriek. The mouse is too terrified to move. The owl grabs the animal in its talons, crushes the mouse's head with its beak, and carries the prey off to a nearby perch for a quick meal.

At one time, a barn owl's eerie cry and ghostly flight caused people to think of this bird as a bad omen. Actually, though, this owl is a farmer's best friend. It eats a lot of small rodents. A barn owl eats as many as three mice a night and more than 1,000 mice a year.

If you come upon a barn owl's nest, the parents may simply fly away, leaving the owlets to fend for themselves. Sometimes the

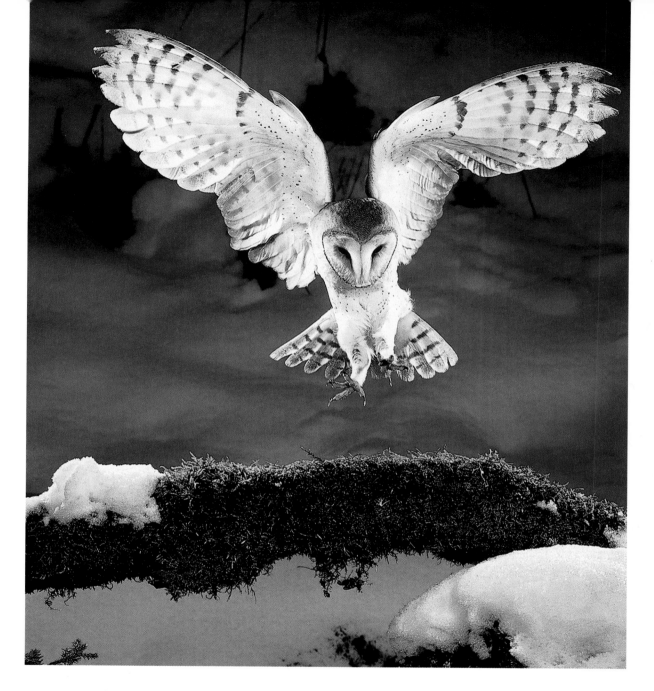

parents will crouch down low, spread their wings, hiss, and snap their bills. If this happens, it's best to sneak away and leave the nestlings alone.

Eared Owls

FAMILY: Strigidae
COMMON EXAMPLE: Short-eared owl
GENUS AND SPECIES: *Asio flammeus*
SIZE: 15 inches (38 cm)

Short-eared owls live in cool places all over the world. In the spring, a male short-eared owl attracts a female by spiraling up into the air, hovering for a few moments, and hooting rapidly. Then he dives down, clapping his wings together loudly. This behavior seems to work—the female usually pays attention.

After the birds mate, the female makes a nest on the ground and lines it with grass and feathers. While she sits on the eggs, the male brings her mouse tidbits. When the owlets finally hatch, the male has even more work to do. He brings mouse after mouse to the female, and she pops the food into the owlets' hungry mouths. Even after the young leave the nest, the parents continue to feed them. It takes about 2 weeks for the birds to learn to fly and hunt.

Short-eared owls usually hunt at night. They swoop over fields, hunting for mice and voles. In one study, scientists found that during a 100-day period, forty owl families living in one area ate close to 50,000 small mammals, mostly meadow mice.

When mice and voles are scarce, short-eared owls lay four or five eggs. When prey is plentiful, however, the owls lay more eggs. During one study, a scientist discovered a nest with fourteen eggs in it.

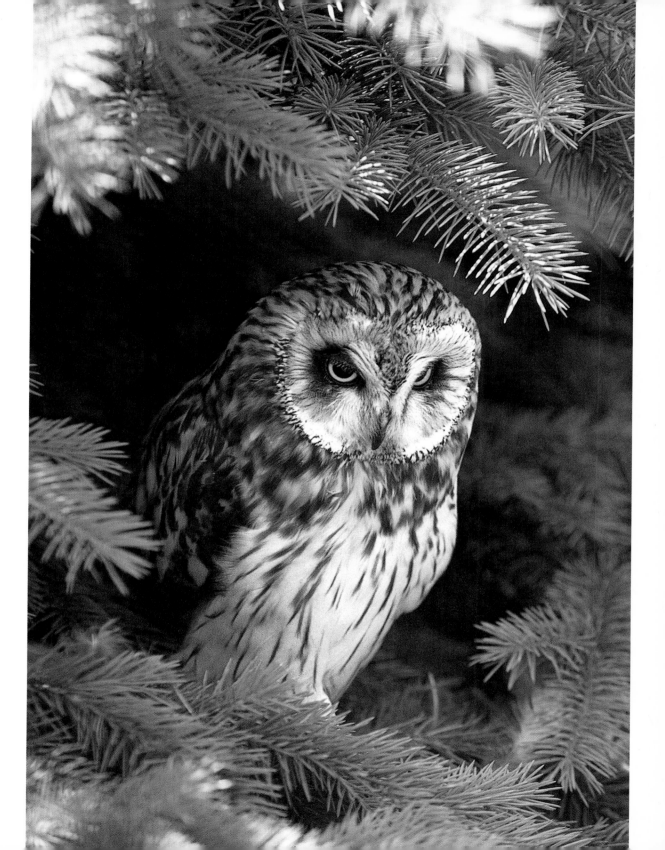

On the Lookout
for Owls

Would you like to see owls for yourself? Finding these secretive birds is not always easy, but if you're quiet—and patient—you may learn to spot them. Before you head out to a field or forest, you'll need binoculars, a journal, a pen, and a field guide to birds.

Since most owls hunt at night, you'll need a pair that works well in twilight hours. Lower-powered binoculars let in more light than high-powered ones, so try to get a 7X (seven-power) pair. When you see something interesting, describe it in your journal. You may even want to draw a few pictures. Be sure to write down the time and your location.

Many owls come out at dusk and perch on trees or posts on the edges of a field. Look for them silhouetted against the sky. Listen for their calls—particularly the "hoo, hoo-hoo, hoo, hoo" of a great horned owl and a barred owl's "Who cooks for YOU? Who cooks for YOU-all?"

Remember that owls have excellent hearing and eyesight. If you see an owl, settle down and be as still and quiet as you possibly can. If you're lucky, you may see the bird take off and swoop down on a mouse.

You can also try to attract an owl by squeaking like a wounded mouse. Crouch down in the grass and try sucking and kissing loudly

A great horned owl perches on a tree branch at dusk.

on your thumb. Pause for awhile to listen and watch, then squeak again. An owl may come flying in to grab what it thinks is easy prey.

You can look for owls roosting during the day too. If you hear crows or jays calling loudly, they may be mobbing an owl. Move— quietly and carefully—toward the racket, and you may see a large, confused owl roosting in a tree. How long do the birds have to mob the owl before it flies away?

You might also see an owl if you look all around you as you creep quietly through the woods. The owl will probably spot you first, but you may see it flying away. If you scare off an owl, it usually doesn't go very far. Move carefully, following its path, and you may see it perching in another tree. Find a hiding place and watch it with your binoculars, but don't go too close. If you scare an owl too often, it may decide to leave for good.

You might also be able to find signs of owls. Look for stick nests high in a tree or tree holes. There may be owlets inside. You can also look for owl feathers, *pellets*, or *whitewash*. Owls eat every bit of their prey, including the bones. They can't digest bones and feathers, though. A few hours after they eat, owls throw up the parts they can't digest in a neat little wad, or pellet.

Great grey owlets in their nest

Whitewash is the name for an owl's thick, white droppings. When an owl has been using a roost for a long time, the whitewash drips down and collects on the lower branches, the tree trunk, and the ground. You can sometimes spot whitewash from quite a distance away. If you find pellets under a whitewashed tree, look up. You may see a roosting owl.

Owls throw up two pellets a day, one at their daytime roost and one at their nighttime feeding spot. If you count the pellets under a tree, you can figure out how long the owl has used the roost. You may want to take the pellets home and pick them apart. The bones, skulls, feathers, and fur can give you an idea of what the owl has been eating.

Spotting owls isn't easy, and it takes a lot of patience, but finding one of these mysterious birds on your own is a wonderful experience.

Can you see the cardinal beak and feathers in this owl pellet?

Words to Know

class—a group of creatures within a phylum that share certain characteristics

court—to try to attract a female for mating

depth perception—the ability to estimate how far away an object is

family—a group of creatures within an order that share certain characteristics

genus (plural **genera**)—a group of creatures within a family that share certain characteristics

kingdom—one of the five divisions into which all living things are placed: the animal kingdom, the plant kingdom, the fungus kingdom, the moneran kingdom, and the protist kingdom

mob—a loud attack that crows and other birds make on roosting owls

order—a group of creatures within a class that share certain characteristics

pellet—a wad of bones, beaks, fur, and other indigestible animal parts that an owl throws up

phylum (plural **phyla**)—a group of animals within a kingdom that share certain characteristics

preening—picking dirt and insects out of feathers

predator—an animal that hunts and eats other animals

prey—an animal that is hunted and eaten by another animal

rodent—a group of small mammals that includes mice, voles, and rats

roost—the spot where a bird sleeps

soil—a mixture of ground up rock and decaying plant and animal matter; it is sometimes called dirt

species—a group of animals within a genus that share certain characteristics. Members of a species can mate and produce young.

talon—one of the sharp claws on the toes of owls and other birds of prey

territory—the area where an animal hunts and raises a family

tundra—a treeless, frozen plain in northern Arctic regions

whitewash—an owl's thick, white droppings

Learning More

Books

Cooper, Ann C., and Joseph Bruchac. *Owls: On Silent Wings*. Niwot, CO: Roberts Rinehart Publishers, 1994.

McKeever, Katherine, and Olena Kassian. *A Place for Owls*. Toronto, Canada: Owl Communications, 1992.

Sattler, Helen R., Jean Day Zallinger, and Helen R. Zallinger. *The Book of North American Owls*. New York: Clarion Books, 1998.

Sutton, Patricia, and Clay Sutton. *How to Spot an Owl*. Shelburne, VT: Chapters Publishing, Ltd., 1996.

Video

Birds of North America, Volume 3, National Audubon Society.

Master Hunter of the Night, Lorne Greene's *New Wilderness* series.

Web Sites

Birdnet
http://www.nmnh.si.edu/BIRDNET/index.html
This site, which is hosted by the Smithsonian Institution for Natural History, provides links to information about all kinds of bird-related subjects.

The Owl Pages
http://www.owlpages.com
This is one of the biggest and best owl sites on the World Wide Web. It is loaded with information, photos, and links to most of the other important owl sites. It also has a good section on owl myths from many different cultures.

Index

About the Author

Sara Swan Miller has enjoyed working with children all her life, first as a nursery-school teacher, and later as an outdoor environmental educator at the Mohonk Preserve in New Paltz, New York. As the director of the Preserve school program, she has led hundreds of children on field trips and taught them the importance of appreciating and respecting the natural world.

She has written a number of children's books, including *Three Stories You Can Read to Your Dog; Three Stories You Can Read to Your Cat; What's in the Woods? An Outdoor Activity Book; Oh, Cats of Camp Rabbitbone!; Piggy in the Parlor and Other Tales; Better Than TV;* and *Will You Sting Me? Will You Bite? The Truth About Some Scary-Looking Insects.* She has also written many other books for the Animals in Order series as well as several books about farm animals for the Children's Press True Books series.